I0482039

Blockchain – The Technology That Is Changing The World

Beginners Guide To The Blockchain Revolution: Investing, Cryptocurrency, Bitcoin, Ethereum - What is it and how does it work?

Table of Contents

Free Bonus Gift!

As a way of saying thank you for purchasing my book, I am adding a FREE 57 page guide titled Cryptocurrency Secrets – offering outstanding value and delving that little bit further into the dizzying potential that the world of cryptocurrency could offer you

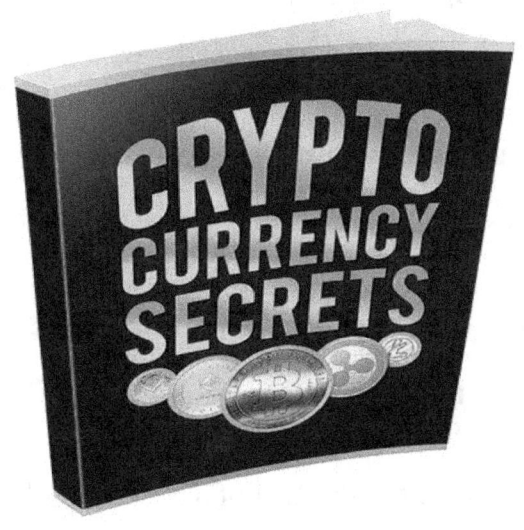

Copy and paste link to grab the free gift!

http://bit.ly/2ngB9cT

Definitions:

Algorithm – a set of mathematical instructions or rules to help calculate an answer to a problem

Altcoins – alternative coin (another cryptocurrency other than Bitcoin)

Bitcoin – a type of digital currency

Block – a permanent store of records which cannot be altered – it is a piece of code which is a predetermined size

Blockchain – a public digital ledger in which transactions are recorded, linked and secured using cryptography

Blockchain scaling – to future proof the technology to scale it up without compromising the security; this has not yet been achieved

Brain Wallets - A **brain wallet** is a method to keep your bitcoin wallet stored only in your mind

Centralization - under the control of a central authority

Centralized Databases - database that is based, stored, and maintained in one location

Chain codes – is a piece of code that is located into a network of that enables interaction with that network's shared ledger.

Cryptocurrency – a digital currency produced by a public network, rather than any government, that uses cryptography to ensure payments are sent and received securely

Cryptography - Cryptography is an area of mathematics concentrating on encryption, security and data protection. Cryptography is the foundation of cryptocurrencies that allows the formation, management and security of the networks to function

Decentralization – to distribute the administrative powers or functions of a central authority over a less concentrated area

Decentralized autonomous organizations - is an organization that is run through rules encoded as computer programs called smart contracts

Decrypt - unlock

Digital wallet - an application or device which allows the user to make payments electronically – it is also a storing place for cryptocurrency. The digital wallet is encrypted

Digital signature - a digital code (created and authenticated by public key encryption) which is attached to an electronically transmitted document to substantiate its contents and the sender's identity

Distributed database - the database consists of multiple, interrelated databases stored at different computer network sites.

Distributed Network - distributed networks and processing work together to deliver specialized applications to different remote users. This means that an application may be hosted and carried out from a single machine but obtained by many others.

Elliptic Curve Cryptography - a public key encryption system based on elliptic curve theory that can be used to create quicker, smaller, and more productive cryptographic keys

Encrypted - to change electronic information or signals into a secret code

Encrypt - lock

Ethereum - is a decentralized platform for applications that run exactly as programmed without any chance of fraud, censorship or third-party interference. Ethereum has its own cryptocurrency called Ether

Genesis Block - this is the first block of a block chain

Hardware wallets - a certain type of bitcoin wallet which stores the user's private keys in a secure hardware device.

Hash – a long and complicated algorithm

Internet of Agreements – uses the blockchain network to transform the domain of global trade and to negate the effects of Brexit and the withdrawal of the United States from the Trans-Pacific Partnership.

Intermediation - brings together inquirer and supplier of goods, information, money, etc.

Internet of Things - is a network of devices that can connect to the web, making normal machines "smart"

Ledger - a book or other collection of financial accounts

Miners - miners are members of the network that confirm the validity of new bitcoin transactions that are waiting to be recorded on a public ledger and decode an encrypted, unique ID, generated by a formula, to add the confirmed records to the blockchain – they do this by allocating computer power in return for a small fee

Node – a computer connected to the network

Nonce – an abbreviation of number used once

Peer-to-peer network - when two or more computer systems are connected and share resources without going through a separate server

Pipe and filter architecture – a very simple, yet powerful architecture, that is also very robust. It consists of any number of components (filters) that convert or filter data, before passing it on via connectors (pipes) to other components

Platform - a group of technologies that are applied as a base with which other applications, processes or technologies are developed

Private blockchains - requires an invitation and must be validated by either the network starter or by a set of rules put in place by the network starter

Private Key – a string of alphanumeric characters that is encrypted – this is known only by the owner. When a user deals with cryptocurrency, he is a given a private key and a public address that can be used to buy or receive tokens or coins. The address is where the funds are credited or debited. If a user does not have a private key, he will not be able to withdraw his coins or tokens from the public address.

Proof of Existence - a service that allows users to upload a file on the network and they need to pay a small transaction fee to obtain a cryptographic proof that it has been added to the blockchain.

Proof of Stake - principle that declares that an individual can mine or validate block transactions according to how many coins they hold. This means that the more cryptocurrency owned by a miner, the more mining power they have.

Proof of Work - is an answer to mathematical puzzle that must be supplied to add a block into the blockchain. The puzzle is tricky to figure out but simple to validate. With cryptocurrencies, it takes a large amount of computing power and resources to produce proof-of-work. Bitcoin uses the SHA-256 hash function. A block is considered valid only if its hash is lower than or equal to the current 256-bit number (target). Each block must contain the hash from the previous block.

Public Blockchain - a blockchain that allows access to anyone. Anybody can gain entry to the blockchain, transact, verify transactions and become part of the process as to which blocks are added to the blockchain. Bitcoin is probably the most widely recognized public blockchain.

Public key – Blockchain equivalent of your bank account number. When you combine the public key and the private key you can access the funds in your wallet. You need to share your public key to receive money into your wallet. To gain access you need to pair it with your private key.

QR Code – Quick Response code – a two-dimensional barcode – can only be read by a device that is set up to read QR codes, for example, a smartphone.

SHA-256 – Secure Hash Algorithm function used to generate a hash. SHA-256 is a 256-bit hash (32-byte character length)

Smart Contract - a computer program that directly regulates the transfer of digital currencies or assets between parties under certain agreed upon conditions

Software wallets – these are termed as 'hot' wallets and are easily connected to the internet. These wallets are ideal if you need frequent access to your tokens.

Timestamp - a digital record of the time of occurrence of an event

Wallet Import Format - is a way of convert a private key to make it easier to copy

51 percent attack – this could happen if more than 50% of the computing power on a cryptocurrency network is controlled by one person or group of people operating together. They could alter the network and blockchain allowing double spending (the same coin or token being spent twice), manipulating transactions and stop transactions from being accepted.

Introduction

Thank you for choosing to download this ebook, *'Blockchains – the technology that is changing the world – what is it and how does it work?*

Blockchain technology, cryptocurrencies, cryptography, Bitcoins, Ethereum, altcoins, private keys and many other terms revolving around digital currency have gained popularity. Some websites have incorporated the blockchain technology and have introduced Bitcoins as a mode of payment. The blockchain technology has taken the world by storm. Every person, including both you and I, have taken an interest to understand the concept of the technology and how it is used to secure cryptocurrencies and transactions made using those currencies.

There is enough material available on the Internet – right from papers to articles written by amateurs – about cryptocurrencies and the blockchain technology. Papers written in the year 1980 introduced the idea of blockchains, and it was in the code for Bitcoins that the blockchain technology was used for the first time. This book covers the history of the blockchain technology and helps you understand how the blockchain works.

Over the course of the book, you will learn about how the blockchain technology is used to secure the Bitcoin network and other cryptocurrency networks. A blockchain keeps the user's funds and identity secure and creates a decentralized network for any transaction to take place.

Owing to the security that the blockchain technology provides, experts are looking at how this technology can be used to enhance some applications in the future. The book covers some applications for the future that can use this technology. The book helps you understand how the technology can be used in those applications. Lastly, you will learn about Bitcoins and how they work. This will help you to begin investing in Bitcoins through the blockchain technology.

Thank you for purchasing the book. I hope you gather all the information you are looking for about the blockchain technology.

Chapter One: A History of Blockchain

There are lots of technologies in today's world that we take for granted which were revolutionary when they were first introduced. Consider the example of smartphones and how they have affected our lives. In earlier times, when a person left home, there was no possible way to call them because there were no mobile phones. However, today, there are people all around the world who build businesses and work entirely on their smartphones. The most astonishing thing is that smartphones have been a part of our lives for just a decade.

Another such revolutionary idea is building around us as we speak. This technology is known as the **blockchain**. Blockchains are widespread and **distributed databases** that maintain a list of transactions or records. Each record is called a **block.**

One of the earliest and most important blockchain innovations is the **Bitcoin** system. Currently, the market cap of the Bitcoin changes between the limits of 15 billion to 20 billion dollars. Today, Bitcoin is used by millions of people around the world for payments.

After Bitcoin became so popular, another innovation known as the blockchain was made. This idea was a realization of the technology that the Bitcoin runs on. The idea was that this technology could be separated from the Bitcoin and used for various other organization problems. Currently, most major financial institutions around the world conduct research on blockchains, and an estimate states that around 20% of the banks will use blockchain by mid-2018.

After this, another novel idea called the **smart contract** was developed. Smart contracts are an upgrade on the blockchain, a "second generation blockchain" if you will. This new system was called **Ethereum**. The major development was that this system introduced small computer programs into the blockchain that allowed for the representation of loans and bonds as opposed to only cash transactions like in Bitcoin. The Ethereum **platform** has an estimated market cap of 1 billion dollars.

The latest innovation in the blockchain domain, which is currently the most cutting-edge technology in the field, is known as **proof of stake**. Blockchains around the world are currently secured by a concept known as **proof of work** wherein the decision makers are the group that possesses the largest computing power. The members of these groups are called **miners**, and they operate vast servers to provide the security. They get paid compensation regarding **cryptocurrency**. The newer systems avoid these types of data centers and introduce financial instruments that provide a higher level of security.

Another novel idea that is on the horizon in the blockchain domain is called **blockchain scaling**. Currently, every computer connected to a blockchain network processes every transaction made on the network. This is obviously a slow process. The idea is to speed-up this process without compromising the security. Determining the number of computers required to process a transaction could do this. This way, the work can be divided easily, and this will accelerate the process. The major obstacle is to figure out a way to do this without affecting the security provided by the network. It is expected that scaled blockchains will be fast enough to support the **Internet of things** and be on par with other payment software such as SWIFT and VISA.

Top scientists, mathematicians and cryptographers around the world have made all these innovations over the past ten years. Once the domain of blockchain hits its maximum potential, the world will be transformed. Transactions across countries, which took days to complete will now take a few hours and eventually just a few minutes. The system of online transactions will be faster and safer than the current structure. There will be self-driving cars and drones that will use the blockchain network to pay for parking spaces.

Another advantage that these technological changes will have is the reduction in transaction costs. Once these transaction costs drop below a certain level, the existing business models will undergo major changes. Such a change happened when the Internet boomed, and it became very easy to reach people around the world. For instance, consider auctions. They used to be very small scale and local. However, once the Internet boomed, sites like eBay allowed auctions to become global events. A similar effect is expected of the blockchain technology.

Predicting the direction that the effect of blockchains will take is difficult. Nobody could have foreseen the boom of social media. Nobody could have guessed that it would become even more popular than watching TV. Most predictions underestimate the long-term effects and overestimate the speed of the changes. However, the current predictions are that the blockchain will have as much impact on the world as the Internet had when it was first introduced. This may not be an exaggeration. One thing for certain is that once the blockchain technology is up and running, it will quickly attract users from all around the world and it will be incorporated into various industries to increase the efficiency of operations. Considering the kind of developments that have been made in the blockchain domain in 10 years, the future of the blockchain could be upon us sooner rather than later.

It was not possible to process credit cards on the Internet until the late 1990s since e-commerce was not invented yet. There are many future projects that are based on the blockchain network. Dubai's blockchain strategy states that all government documents need to be issued on the blockchain by the year 2020. An idea called the **Internet of Agreements** was presented at the World Government Summit, and this idea uses the blockchain network to transform the domain of global trade and to negate the effects of Brexit and the withdrawal of the United States from the Trans-Pacific Partnership. All these ideas are great in theory and need to be tested practically. However, in Dubai, it is expected that the savings from the blockchain network will easily cover the cost of the project and will easily be covered by the savings that are produced by the blockchain network.

Chapter Two: An Introduction to

Blockchains

The meaning of a blockchain

A blockchain is very similar to a **ledger**. It is essentially a decentralized and digitized ledger that can be accessed by the public. The blockchain grows every time a new transaction is made. Each transaction is called a block, and these blocks get added in chronological order to the blockchain. Since this is available to the public, the people can access it without any central control. Every computer that is connected to the network is called a **node**, and each node is given access to the blockchain.

The idea of blockchain was first implemented for the cryptocurrency Bitcoin. As mentioned earlier, the blockchain was realized only after Bitcoin was up and running. It uses a distributed ledger technology, and it is currently being implemented in various other domains as well. As of today, the blockchain technology is primarily used for digital currencies and verifying the transactions made using digital currencies. However, it is very easy to use computer codes to insert any document into the blockchain. The blockchain records all transactions, and no one can edit these.

Going deeper into a blockchain

Blockchains are made up of blocks, and each block is the current section of the chain. This block keeps track of a few recent transactions that have been made. Once done, the block is added to the blockchain where it can never be edited. Whenever a block is added to the chain, a new one is generated. There are millions of such blocks that are linked to each other in a fixed, chronological order. The first block of a blockchain is called the **genesis block**. Each block contains a reference that points to the previous block. The chain holds information about various user addresses and contains their balances.

The design of the blockchain was such that the transactions recorded on it could not be modified or deleted. This is the case because the transactions are added using **cryptography**. The data can be shared across the world, but it cannot be copied. However, the problem with the blockchain is that it is constantly growing. This could lead to issues such as a lack of storage space.

Blockchains and the Bitcoin platform

As mentioned earlier the blockchain is the underlying technology that the Bitcoin platform runs on. One of the biggest advantages of the blockchain technology is that it removes the need for a third party to validate the transactions. When one user makes a payment to another, the two parties involved need to validate it. This transaction is then added to a public record and attached to the blockchain. Once in the blockchain, various other users of the platform will access the transaction and verify or nullify it. Studies have shown that a new block is added to the blockchain every 8 minutes through the process of mining.

According to the Bitcoin protocol, the blockchain along with all its transactions are open to all users on the network. The moment a computer is added to the network, it receives a copy of the entire blockchain, which holds information about

21

every transaction that has been executed. Users can access the blockchain to obtain information about the value that a certain user had at a point.

Extensions of Blockchains

Let us look at an analogy of a conventional bank. The blockchain is essentially like a complete history of the bank's transactions. Each block in the chain is a separate bank statement. However, a major difference between the blockchain and the complete history of a bank's transactions is that the former is distributed. This characteristic helps in making the operations of the involved parties easier. This is the main reason why many other fields such as the Internet of Things and insurance agencies are trying to adopt the blockchain technology into their functionality. Supporters of the blockchain technology believe that this distributed ledger system can be used in other areas such as voting systems, medical records, auctioning, vehicle registrations and many more.

Many people around the world have noticed the potential of the distributed ledger technology to make operations of companies easier. Due to this, many new business models based on the blockchain technology are being designed to replace the current models that use bookkeeping methods for transaction history. The technology is so easy to work with that it could save companies a huge amount of money: a recent study by Goldman Sachs showed that the blockchain technology could cut costs of stock market operators by up to 6 billion dollars per annum.

The initial fears about the blockchain technology were that it might not be secure enough and that could lead to frauds taking place. However, after institutions have considered it further, they realized that it provided high security and can also help in cutting costs. Another added advantage is that the system is much faster.

The first international transaction on the blockchain network was completed on October 24th of 2016. Wells Fargo & Company and the Commonwealth Bank of Australia brokered this. It was a deal worth 35,000 dollars, which involved Brigham Cotton, an Australian cotton trader, which bought 88 bales of cotton from the United States division in Texas and shipped them to Qingdao in China.

Advantages of a Blockchain

As mentioned earlier, the blockchain platform has numerous advantages and business benefits. Most of these are based on providing users with at least one of the following:

Efficiency

Since the network does not require a third party to intervene and only the two parties involved take part in the transaction, these transactions can be completed quickly. In addition to this, the users can operate through smart contracts which allow the users to trigger transactions on satisfying the terms and conditions of the contract. This can go a long way in streamlining the process and can, therefore, save time and money.

Auditability

Since each transaction on the blockchain is recorded in chronological order, there exists an unchangeable transaction trail associated with an asset. This becomes very important when the authenticity of an asset is to be verified using source data. The company Everledger uses this characteristic to track diamonds.

Traceability

The blockchain network can be easily used to track a product. It can help when a user is looking to track where some assets are currently. Information can then be exchanged between the user and the owner of the asset. This aspect of the blockchain network is reviewed and discussed in the article, "Global Supply Chains Are About to Get Better, Thanks to Blockchain."

Transparency

There have been numerous occasions in the past where relations have broken down due to a lack of transparency. This can also lead to delays in transactions between two parties. The blockchain network is characterized by transparency, and this helps in building trust between users on the network and can, therefore, build stable relationships as well.

Security

Authenticity and security of the information on the network are assured since users within the network verify all transactions. The verification is done using complex cryptography. This assurance of information is essential to facilitating the use of IoT (Internet of Things). The Internet of Things is a cyber autonomous process within a closed loop that links actions to assets. There is an article titled, "Securing 3D Printing: Could Blockchain be the Answer?" which talks about a version of IoT that is being used for protection and verification of IP.

Feedback

Since there is complete traceability for an asset on the blockchain network, manufacturers and designers of assets can absorb management of assets into these assets to make them useful. The network also allows for easy communication between customers and manufacturers and therefore the process of giving feedback becomes easier.

Chapter Three: Understanding the

Blockchain Technology

The blockchain network is undoubtedly an amazing invention. It was invented as the technology underlying the Bitcoin network, which was created by Satoshi Nakamoto. However, once people realized how effective it is and separated it from the Bitcoin network, it has evolved into something much greater.

The blockchain network gave rise to a new kind of Internet where information in the digital form can be distributed between users but not copied. It was originally designed only for the cryptocurrency Bitcoin. However, many people have noticed its potential, and it is now being implemented in various other walks of life.

In the world of cryptocurrency, Bitcoin is called digital gold and this name is not an overstatement. The total value of all the Bitcoins in circulation hit a record of 14 billion US dollars in the past week. The blockchain network can have other types of digital value. You do need to know how the blockchain network works to use it. However, it does not hurt to have an idea about the network since it is quite interesting to read about. The focus of this book is to provide you with this basic knowledge. From a very outer level, the blockchain network looks a lot like Wikipedia and other networks you may be familiar with.

When it comes to the blockchain network, different users can make entries into the network. There exists a community of users (called miners in the Bitcoin network) that have the power to edit or update the entries. Comparing this to

Wikipedia, the entries on Wikipedia are not controlled by a single user either.

When we delve further into the details of the blockchain network, the characteristics that make it unique become more obvious. The blockchain network and Wikipedia both run on **distributed networks**. The latter is incorporated into the World Wide Web through a client-server model. Users are known as clients, and each user has a specific set of permissions that allow them to edit entries on Wikipedia. All these entries are stored on a central server.

Whenever a user tries to use Wikipedia, any page that they request access for will be the updated version. Any changes that have been made are updated and then displayed. However, the entire database of entries is controlled by a group of Wikipedia administrators that have authority on the permissions available to the users.

The backbone that Wikipedia runs on is very similar to the centralized databases that banks, insurance companies, and governments use today. These databases provide high security. However, when it comes to **centralized databases**, the control lies completely in the hands of the owners. The owners have power over all the edits, updates and permissions that users have.

The blockchain technology, on the other hand, runs on a distributed database. The main difference is that this database is not centralized. This is the most important and characterizing feature of the blockchain network. Every Wikipedia page has what is called a master copy, which exists on the main server. All edits are made to this copy, and this is what gets displayed to users. However, in a blockchain network, all computers connected to the network update the various blocks independently. The version of the block that is most popular becomes the official copy of the block. Every time a transaction is performed on the network, it gets broadcast, and all the nodes on the network update the blockchain.

This is another important feature of the blockchain network. This means that there is no need for a third party to verify transactions and update the records. It also depicts a new style of storing information and distributing it. However, blockchain is not a novel idea. It is just a mixture of various other technologies that are being applied in new styles. It is a combination of three proven technologies, namely, the Internet, a protocol that helps in governing incentivization and private key cryptography. The result of the mixture of these three technologies is a new network that allows for digital interactions between users without the intervention of an outside party. The network provides security to its users and their information as well.

What exactly is Digital Trust?

It is extremely difficult to define the word trust. It can be a judgment of risk between different people. When it comes to the digital world, trust between two parties almost always comes down to verifying identity and permissions. In layman's terms, trust can be built using two questions: "Is your identity the same as the one you say it is?" and "Do you have the permission to perform the activities you are currently performing?"

This authentication process is completed by the **private key** cryptography that is a key component of the blockchain network. Every user on the network possesses a private key, and this represents ownership. Since the private key is the only requirement for ownership, it does not require users to divulge any other personal information on the network, and this protects from hackers and identity thefts.

The distributed nature of the blockchain network helps in reducing the risk of corruption and failure of the system. On a centralized system, if the main server crashes, the entire system shuts down until repair. However, in the blockchain network, even if a single node shuts down, the other nodes can continue to use the network.

The blockchain network also has a protocol that all users must follow. This protocol helps in maintaining the network's security and order. Only when the rules of the protocol are followed, do transactions get recorded and updated on the network.

All these characteristics of the network allow for the building of stable digital relationships that are not completely dependent on trust. This is very attractive to many entrepreneurs in various industries. The lack of requirement of expensive trust is a very eye-catching quality of the blockchain network. This network is extremely conducive for transactions across the Internet. In fact, many people are calling it the transaction layer on the Internet- the Internet of Value.

The notion that private cryptographic keys and public ledgers which record all the information can provide users with the incentive to create digital relationships is yet another attractive characteristic of the network. Many companies from different industries are looking to build this network. The configuration of the network automatically establishes the authenticity of all users and provides the permissions to them.

How does the blockchain network maintain security?

As already mentioned, the blockchain technology was not designed separately. It was designed along with the Bitcoin network. However, the blockchain technology could easily prove to be more valuable than the Bitcoin. However, its value lies entirely in its security. So, as we start setting up the technology, we need to make sure that the starting configurations for the technology are not going to lead to security issues in the future. To make sense of the possible security problems in a blockchain, it is first important to learn the differences between private and public blockchains.

The Bitcoin network is a **public blockchain**. This is a network where all users connected to the network can view the transactions or even add more. Anybody on the network can perform transactions and add them to the public ledger. To do this they need to solve a complicated cryptographic puzzle, and this shows that the person is trying to make the transaction happen. This prevents hackers from incorporating a virus into the network that can record fake transactions. A consensus protocol is followed to confirm and verify transactions on the network. On the Bitcoin network, there is no single user who is tasked with verifying all the transactions. Miners do this job by solving the cryptographic puzzles, and they are compensated in the form of Bitcoins. The user who solves the puzzle the fastest is paid.

The characteristics of freedom of access to records and decentralization have provided some unforeseen consequences. Since anybody can access and update transactions on the Bitcoin network, black market transactions have become a common occurrence. Since the process of mining requires large amounts of electricity, most miners work from countries that have cheap electricity. This essentially leads to a centralization of the network and could lead to collusion. Changes in electricity prices across the world can lead to changes in the working of the network. Therefore, most people are looking for **private blockchains** for their enterprises.

In private blockchains, the owners of the networks have control over which users can submit transactions to the ledgers, access the ledgers or verify the transactions in them. The main use of private blockchains can be marketed in which various parties operate simultaneously, but trust is not established. Private blockchains can provide security since it removes the risk of a black market forming. It cannot be said for sure that there would never be security issues on private blockchains. However, they remove most of the risks that are associated with public blockchains, and this is a step in the right direction.

Chapter Four: Decentralization

One of the main themes in the shift from **pipe architecture** too is **decentralization**. Pipe models relied on **centralization** of the network. The networks were built on supply chains that were owned and managed through contracts. Platform architectures decentralized this ownership.

The platforms around the world today such as Airbnb, Uber, and Trivago all have one characteristic in common: they are all decentralized networks wherein the ownership does not lie in any one system. The exchanges made on these networks are called decentralized exchanges. By keeping the supply low and the demand high, the industry was able to maintain control over the exchanges and therefore made it difficult for people to become drivers. Uber circumvented this and allowed anybody to become a driver and work on the platform.

Even though the transactions on Uber are decentralized, the company still has a large amount of control on the platform. Uber does this by owning the identity of the users of the platform, the payment mechanisms, the pricing of the service, the logistics involved and the rules that govern the service. Most importantly, Uber has the power to control the openness provided by the platform since the company acts as an intermediary in the transactions. As a centralized intermediary, Uber can pose all the threats that have been posed by other intermediaries while regulating the markets. This is how the blockchain network can help in creating a new model of **intermediation** on platforms.

There are many definitions and interpretations of the blockchain network, but there are two important features that are attractive to entrepreneurs and governments. The network is a **peer-to-peer network** that allows a distributed community to verify or update transactions and other interactions. Secondly, the governance of the transactions is managed by using a decentralized ledger that runs on a distributed system with a consensus protocol, which makes it next to impossible to commit fraud.

What are intermediaries and what are the associated risks?

Traditionally, intermediaries around the world such as financial institutions, governments, banks and other policymakers played the role of advisors. Their main job was to create a set of rules and protocols that would develop the trust of the customers, and all the transactions would operate based on these protocols. These institutions became necessary when the world moved from local market economies to industrial economies that are dictated by capital. While everyone looked to the intermediary institutions to develop trust and ensure proper functioning of the market, there are quite a few instances in history where intermediaries have failed at this job and have led to a disaster in the market. An example of these instances is the financial crisis in 2008 where the entire economy collapsed because the banks gave loans to people with very low credit rating and many people ended up defaulting on these house loans.

As these new platforms are being introduced in the economy, a massive consolidation is being observed in the markets in which platforms work on the winner takes all principle. This trend is not seen in all markets, but it has been noticed that many platforms have benefited on national and international scales. As these platforms increase in size as intermediaries in the market, they can extend in a manner that affects the rest of the market that depends on them. Recently, Uber had increased its commission for the drivers from 20 to 25 percent. This hurt the income of drivers of private enterprises. This incident brought to light the risks of depending on platform intermediaries.

Models of governance based on blockchains

This risk is being addressed (attempting to be addressed if you will) by blockchain startups around the world. Blockchains allow you to write code for any required functionality and to then deploy it on all systems connected to the network. Therefore, the functionality of an intermediary can be coded, and this code can then be deployed onto all the distributed computers connected to the network. Also, blockchains provide high certainty that the deployed code will function in the same manner across different systems all the time. This unique characteristic of the blockchain makes it conducive to generate a new model of platform governance. Blockchains take the rudimentary blocks required for a platform and then distribute them across various systems. This shift is still in its infancy, but this is a sign that the world will switch to using decentralized intermediaries.

Chapter Five: Ten Rules to never break in a

Blockchain

This chapter focuses on a few rules to follow when working with a blockchain network or any of the cryptocurrencies that are run on them. Make sure that you consult your attorney or any trusted advisor before you start using them for financial purposes. These systems are relatively new, and the rules that govern them are vague.

Do not use a blockchain to break the law

As you probably know, cryptocurrencies are not legal everywhere in the world at this point. Therefore, you need to make sure that you do not break the law when working with them.

- A very common question that neophytes in the world of cryptocurrency ask is, "Can you use cryptocurrency to hide money?" This is a very dangerous notion to think of. Blockchain networks keep track of every transaction ever made on them. Even if you can conjure up a smart way to hide the use of currency somewhere, a person who has time and is looking for malpractice can easily sniff it out.
- Another important thing to keep in mind is never to use the blockchain network to smuggle money across international borders. Many countries have rules on how much money can be carried across their borders. Blockchains keep a record of every transaction made so smuggling money across borders is a big no.

- Some people believe that cryptocurrency can be used to buy goods on the black market. Again, since there is a record of any transaction, this would be a very bad idea.

Maintain simplicity in your transactions

Currently, some of the most cutting-edge technology around the world are smart contracts, **chain codes** and **decentralized autonomous organizations** (DAOs). Lots of corporations around the world are attracted by the reduced administration and costs by adopting blockchain networking. One thing that some people tend to forget is that this is simply computer code. This means that there is no human governing body, which is ensuring that everyone on the network is following the rules that have been laid out. The code is the law and so whatever is incorporated into the code becomes law. Human intervention might be required at times.

Since there is no human that can interpret the computer code, when the code starts to function abnormally, there is no way for a user to notice it or report it to an authority. So, it is a good idea to keep your transactions simple so that you can predict the outcome of your transaction and therefore check if the rules are being followed. Remember that there is no human intervention that is possible, so you are responsible for your transactions obeying or disobeying the rules.

Publish records of your transactions with caution

As mentioned earlier, one of the main features of the blockchain is that once a transaction is recorded, it is next to impossible to delete it from the ledger. Therefore, it will be present in the record books for a long time. Suppose you upload some sensitive data in an encrypted format on the blockchain, someone someday might manage to break the encryption and read the data that you uploaded.

Currently, there is work being conducted in the field of cryptography regarding the subject of **quantum proof encryption**. However, since quantum proof encryption and quantum computing are still in their early stages, no predictions can be made on how effective these technologies will be in the future.

Store all your private keys somewhere (back them up)

The strict rules of blockchain networks can sometimes be unforgiving. You cannot retrieve private keys if you lose them or request a change when you forget them. If this happens, all the money and data that you had stored on the blockchain will be lost, and you will never be able to retrieve them until you can remember your key.

These keys for cryptocurrencies are generally inside the wallets. It is extremely important that you secure them and keep them safe at all costs. Do not store your money in online services and cryptocurrency exchanges for too long. Many exchanges have lost money in the past, and there is nothing you can do to retrieve the stolen money.

Keep your private keys and other currency in cold storage away from the Internet. Write down all your private keys and store them somewhere safe and do not let anyone else know the location. This may sound like a dramatic statement, but you would be smart to follow it.

Before confirming a transaction, verify the address of the recipient

The world of cryptocurrency and blockchain networks has a significant number of unscrupulous individuals who are looking to steal your data and currency. Be very careful in sharing your data. As soon as it is uploaded onto the network, it is going to stay there for a long time. You cannot pull it back so make sure you verify the data.

When you are sending money to someone, double check the address of the recipient. If you put the wrong address and confirm it, the only way you can retrieve the money is if the recipient sends it back by themselves. The only problem is that you cannot access their personal information. So, make sure the address is correct.

When you are using the exchanges, take extreme caution

Exchanges for cryptocurrencies that run on blockchain networks are focal points of attacks from hackers. Many hackers attack them to steal easy money, and over 150 exchanges have been successfully stolen from.

Keep this in mind when you are dealing with cryptocurrency exchanges. Read up online for the rules to keep your money safe. Research the exchange that you are looking to use to know more about its security precautions.

Lastly, remember to use these exchanges only to move your money in and out. Do not store any money on them. Store the cryptocurrencies on some paper or in cold storage and keep many copies of the keys.

Take caution with the Wi-Fi

When you are using the network, make sure that your router is set up correctly. If it is not, there is a possibility that someone else can see your activity log. If you are using a public network, the owner of the network can easily access your log.

Research your blockchain development

Since blockchain technology is new, there are very few people around the world who have a lot of experience working with it or building applications that run on it.

Before approaching someone to help you build a blockchain network for your application, look up their profiles to see if they are reliable architects of the network. Even if the person is not specifically experienced with blockchain networks, make sure that they have had a lot of experience with developing similar networks other than blockchains.

Another problem is that there are not many resources or manuals on the Internet that can help developers when they get stuck at some point. So, take it for granted that the building of the network will take a while. However, hiring someone with experience in the field of networks might expedite the process.

Don't get fooled by the network

For a long time now, humans have used banks and other financial institutions as intermediaries for their transactions. So, we are used to the rules and regulations that govern the banks. The blockchain network does not have the same type of security or rules and regulations. There is no customer service and consumer protection. When money is lost in your bank, there is always some procedure that can be followed to retrieve the money. However, if you lose money on a blockchain network, there may be no way that you can use to get it back.

Another thing to consider is that there has been a lot of hype surrounding block chains in the past few years, but there have not been any results. In the year of 2016, there were nearly a 1000 new blockchain companies that proclaimed they were experts at building the network. Although there is a lot of hype surrounding it, before investing in a blockchain network, take some time to think about it to see if it makes any sense. Think about the following questions:

- Has the technology shown any real results yet?
- Are the results that have been generated helping you?
- Are there other technologies out there that can serve the same purpose that has been well tested?

We do not deny that there is a lot of promise in the technology of blockchain networks. However, it would be advisable to tread carefully until some results of real value have been shown.

Do not use the network unless you are sure of what you are doing

One of the major disadvantages of blockchain networks is that they can be unpredictable. Cryptocurrencies specifically are extremely volatile, and their value can change rapidly at any point in time. Most of these currencies have trends that make no sense and investing large amounts of money could cause you to lose a large amount of money.

Similarly, when it comes to uploading data, be very careful that you are uploading the right data. As mentioned earlier, once it is on the network, pulling the data off will be impossible, and anyone can access it and read it. When it comes to money, before trading in cryptocurrencies, research the market well and then proceed with caution.

Chapter Six: Limitations of Blockchain

When it comes to any new and revolutionary technology, there will always be the doubters along with the supporters. Many people have stated that the blockchain technology is overhyped and that there are lots of limitations and therefore it is doomed to fail in the future. Although there are certain limitations, it cannot be said for sure that the technology would fail. Through trial and error, the blockchain technology could surmount its limitations and become a huge success. Given below are some of the limitations of the technology.

The technology can be too complex to understand initially

The blockchain technology has many new terms that can be confusing to new users. There is too much technical jargon involved, and this could discourage some people from entering the domain. However, efforts are being made to provide glossaries and indexes that have a list of the words and their meanings.

Network size

Like other distributed systems, blockchain networks are not exactly resistant to outside threats. They are, on the other hand, systems that learn from attacks and become more resistant. They mutate whenever they are under threat. However, for this quality to be true, the network needs to be massive. There needs to be a huge number of nodes on the network to make it more robust and resistant to threats.

Many of the skeptics of blockchain networks have said that this is a major flaw in the system since a large network of nodes cannot be guaranteed.

Transaction costs and network speed

Although Bitcoin was almost free to use in its first few years, it has recently become quite expensive regarding transaction costs. A study was conducted in 2016, and it was seen that the Bitcoin network could only process seven transactions in one second and could store about 80 bytes of data. Additionally, each transaction costs about 20 cents. Another issue with the network is that it is being used as a storage of information. This could lead to the requirement of large amounts of storage space, and miners take issue with this because they need to keep reprocessing the information. The additional information stored on the network could further slow it down as well.

Possibility of human error

If a blockchain is developed primarily as a database, the information that is being stored in it needs to be of good quality. Since any data can be stored in the database, it is not trustworthy in and of itself. All data uploads need to be accurately recorded. If garbage data is inputted into the database, the database will output garbage data as well, and this could lead to malfunctioning.

Security flaws may arise

There exists a massive flaw regarding security with blockchain networks, and it is called the **51 percent attack**. A 51 percent attack is an occurrence where if more than half of the nodes on a blockchain network input the same false data, that false data is considered true by the network. Satoshi Nakamoto highlighted this when he initially launched the Bitcoin network. Due to this, the community monitors the mining pools in the Bitcoin network so that nobody can gain power over the network.

Chapter Seven: Private and Public keys

If you have read papers about Bitcoins or other types of cryptocurrencies, you will have come to the terms public and private keys. This chapter covers all the information about public and private keys.

Private Keys 101

A user will need a private key, which is a form of cryptography, which will allow him or her to access their cryptocurrency. This key is a crucial aspect of **altcoins** and Bitcoins since its security helps to protect the user from unauthorized access to the cryptocurrency and theft.

When a user deals with cryptocurrency, he is a given a private key and a **public address** that can be used to buy or receive tokens or coins. The address is where the funds are credited or debited. If a user does not have a private key, he will not be able to withdraw his coins or tokens from the public address. A public key is created from a private key using a complex mathematical **algorithm** that makes it impossible to reverse the generation of a **public key** from a private key.

A private key is made of alphanumeric characters – 51 in number – making it difficult for a hacker to crack. A public address could be compared with a mailbox, and the private key is like the key to that box. Anybody can send letters or small packages to the owner of the mailbox through the opening, but the only person who can obtain the contents of the mailbox is the person who owns the key. Therefore, it becomes imperative that the owner keeps the key safely. If someone were to steal the key, all the information in the mailbox could be compromised.

The private key for any user is stored in a **digital wallet**. Once a transaction is initiated, during the processing of the transaction using the private key, the software in the digital wallet creates a **digital signature**. This signature upholds the security of the system since it confirms that the transaction is taking place between two users. It ensures that any transaction cannot be reversed or changed once it has been broadcasted. If the transaction is changed slightly, the digital signature will also need to change, and this is done within the digital wallet itself.

A user cannot access his or her digital wallet or make any transactions if he or she loses their private key. It is essential that a user saves his or her private key. There are many ways to store a private key in a digital wallet. Private keys can also be printed with a **QR code** and the key, which can be scanned when a transaction is made. These keys are stored on paper wallets and are used as signatures to sign off on transactions.

Private keys can be stored on **hardware wallets**. These wallets use USB devices or smartcards to create and secure a private key offline. A user could also choose to use offline **software wallets** to store his or her private key. The wallet has a partition that is used to store private keys. This partition is only used when the device is offline. Offline software wallets also have an online division where public keys are stored. In such wallets, a transaction is first moved offline to obtain the digital signature after which it is moved back online and broadcasted on the network.

The types of storage addressed above are commonly known as cold storage systems since private keys are stored offline.

Another type of wallet, called a hot wallet, stores a private key on a system or device only when it is connected to the Internet. For example, these wallets include mobile wallets like Xapo, desktop wallets like MultiBit, and web-based wallets like Coinbase.

Things to know about Private Keys

Now that you have gathered all the information about private keys let us look at six things every person must know about private keys.

Private Keys are Just Numbers

Private keys that are generated by wallets are integers between the range 1 – 1077. This may seem like an exhaustive selection but is infinite concerning the use of the integers in the range.

It would take years to process the number of private keys that are in the Bitcoin network which is a property that is key to securing transactions in the Bitcoin network. Since private keys comprise of many numbers, especially when expressed in a decimal format, an alternative format called WIF (**Wallet Import Format**) was devised. In this format, every private key contains alphanumeric characters and starts with the number five. Consider the following WIF representation:

5KJvsngHeMpm884wtkJNzQGaCErckhHJBGFsvd3VyK5q MZXj3hS

Since private keys are supposed to be kept secure, they are often **encrypted** by the system. Some methods include the creation of strings in the same format as that of a WIF private key, but beginning with the number 6. When a private key is first encrypted, the user is given a password, which will need to be used to decrypt the private key.

Private Keys are Signatures

Every transaction that is made using any cryptocurrency bears a digital signature. As the private key, the digital signature is also selected from a large range of integers. Most wallets have software that generates a digital signature using mathematical algorithms. These algorithms create a signature that is synonymous with the private key involved in the transaction.

This system is secure since people involved in the transaction can use the signature to verify if the message is authentic. A digital signature cannot be faked or recreated since it is created only when the private key involved in the transaction is accurate.

A digital signature will change if the transaction has been altered, even if it is a small change made. It is impossible to predict how the signature may change which secures the transaction since the user will be the only one to know what the signature is. This is true because a digital signature is created using a private key.

You must note that the format of a transaction is not as important as the digital signature that is created for the transaction. This is because a signature can be used to check the authenticity of the transaction. You can gather more information about transactions from the Internet.

Private keys can be used to steal

The Bitcoin network and blockchain technology will accept a transaction that bears a valid digital signature. A person who possesses a private key can create a digital signature thereby creating a valid transaction. This means that a person who knows your private key can steal from your digital accounts.

Thieves and hackers have identified different ways to steal private keys, and two of the most common channels are communication channels and storage media. It is for this reason that a user will need to be cautious when he or she stores or transmits his or her private key.

If a user were to use a software wallet, his private key is at risk. A software wallet stores all private keys on the main hard drive of the wallet in a "wallet file." This file is then stored in a well-known directory that is accessible to numerous thieves and hackers.

To overcome this vulnerability, software wallets allow the user to encrypt the wallet file. The hacker would first need to decrypt the wallet file to access the private key. It gets difficult for the hacker if the user makes use of a strong password and a good encryption code. A user could use many software wallets to encrypt the wallet file. All he or she would need to do is maintain a strong password.

Wallet backups are good ideas, but they can result in private keys being leaked. For instance, you may choose to save your private key on the cloud by using Dropbox or Apple Cloud. There are numerous people who can access the cloud and look at the backup, and they can use your private key to access your funds. A similar problem can arise if you send the private key via email or leave a copy of the key around the house. You can choose to encrypt your keys, but this does not eliminate the risk. Cold storage is the safest way to store your private key since that secures the keys better.

Addresses are derived from public keys which are derived from private keys

A public key is created through mathematical algorithms using the private key. These algorithms are defined in the **Elliptic Curve Cryptography** (ECC). A public key consists of two integers while a private key consists of only one integer. If the system preferred to use a public key, it would need to identify a way to transform the two integers into one. For example, the uncompressed public key approach uses mathematical algorithms to add the y-coordinate to the x-coordinate.

The relationship between a private and public key is a classic example of mathematical trapdoors. It is simple to perform the function in one direction and impossible to perform the same function in the reverse direction. It is for this reason that the blockchain technology is secure.

Like private keys, public keys can also be shortened to make them usable with keyboards and displays. Applying transformations to public keys creates addresses. These transformations produce a string of alphanumeric characters that start with the number 1.

A network is often not required to generate a private key or the address. Any system in the Bitcoin network is aware of the relationship that exists between private and public keys that enables the user to choose private keys and digital signatures to make transactions on the network. This ensures that any key that is selected correctly is unique.

Always choose the right private key to maintain security

A user will only need to be aware of his private key to make transactions on the Bitcoin network. It is imperative that he or she keep their private key safe. However, a user's funds could be vulnerable if he or she was careless when it comes to selecting a private key.

Often, a user prefers to generate a private key that is easy to remember. Let us assume that the user wants to choose a valid private key starting with the number 1. How secure do you think this private key would be? The number 1 generates the following private key:

1EHNa6Q4Jz2uvNExL497mE43ikXhwF6kZm

If you were to follow the link, you would find that this address is involved in 2,000 transactions for 7 BTC in a span of a few years. Since you know the private key, you can make transactions using the funds present in this address. You are not willing to hack into another address and steal funds, but what if this address was available to a hacker? He could choose to list down the private keys that are easy to remember and generate addresses for all those keys and constantly monitor the transactions that take place with those addresses. If a fund does arrive at the address, the hacker can then transfer those funds immediately to another account.

If a user were to choose a private key using a random number generator, the hacker would never be able to use the above method. He would need to resort to brute force to hack into the address, which is impossible for any person to achieve.

But, what happens when the random number generator does not generate numbers at random? For instance, what if the private keys generated were clustered around a constant value?

A hacker who was aware of such a defect in the generator can reduce the search space. This would give him the opportunity to monitor all addresses that are based on the faulty generator and steal funds from any address generated with ease. It is for this reason that a strong private key will need to be selected by the user. Using **brain wallets** can do this. A brain wallet uses a passphrase that is then run through a mathematical function to generate a random number and then a private key. Consider the following passphrase "to be or not to be," and the algorithm SHA-256. The algorithm generates the following address using the passphrase:

1J3m4nneGFppRjx6qv92qyz7EsMVdLfr8R

If you click on the link, you will notice that this address was last used in 2016 to make transactions and the funds were withdrawn immediately. It is difficult to identify which passphrase qualifies as secure for a brain wallet. A hacker can exploit this vulnerability and steal funds. It becomes easier for a hacker to exploit funds from generated addresses if the user is an amateur. A hacker can make a list of common passphrases and passwords being used. This list could have close to trillions of entries making it easy for the hacker to use algorithms to generate addresses and private keys.

Let us look at the difference between the situation above and a website password. Your website password could be the same as that of another person. However, you cannot take over their account since you have unique usernames. This is not the case for private keys since they serve a dual role — they are used to create user addresses and digital signatures.

Private keys are secure when they are generated with unpredictability. This ensures that any hacker or thief does not guess the keys.

Private Keys are Portable

Wallet software often hides the process of creating, storing, and using a private key. But, there are times when a private key becomes visible. At such an instance, it becomes important to understand a private key and how it interacts with the software your wallet uses.

Private keys could be released or leaked easily if the user were to use a paper wallet. Paper wallets do come in different formats, but the important feature of a paper wallet is to print a private key and store it as a hard copy.

Most software wallets support sweeping which helps to create a new transaction that pays an existing address in the software wallet. This could empty the funds in the address that is associated with that private key. It is important to understand how you can lose money through private keys in the Bitcoin network.

If the wallet application you use begins to malfunction, then a private key can be imported using an external application. This process provides hackers with another route to access your private key. One way to restore a private key is by using a backup file.

Chapter Eight: Applications of Blockchains

for the future

So, by now, you are aware of all the upsides and limitations of the blockchain network. You probably realize the great potential that it has as well. However, how exactly can the technology be applied to various industries? Up until now, cryptocurrencies have been running on these networks, but the fact of the matter is that there are other applications as well. Given below are a few of the applications that are currently being worked on:

Distributed Cloud Storage

It was mentioned earlier that one of the most important features of the blockchain network is that it is a distributed system. Due to this feature, blockchain data storage will soon become a large-scale disruptor. The cloud storage services around the world are centralized. Therefore, all users of the cloud must trust a single server farm to store all their data. Blockchain technology will help decentralize this. A company called Storj is currently beta-testing a cloud storage concept using a blockchain-powered network to improve security.

Another idea for the future is that users can lend their extra storage space (like Airbnb) to other users. Other users can use your storage space to store their data at an agreed price. Encrypting data and storing it in different locations can help in securing it.

Digital Identity

One of the major threats to people who use the Internet often is identity theft. Imagine a world where you would never have to worry about digital security. According to a report by Distil Networks, identity theft is estimated to cost the industry a whopping 18.5 billion dollars every year.

Blockchain technologies help in making managing digital identities and tracking them secure and an efficient process. This helps in reducing fraud. When it comes to national security, banking, online retailing, or citizenship documentation, identity authentication, and authorization is something that is embedded in culture worldwide.

Let us look at an example of the company Target. There was a data breach at Target, and it was much worse than what was reported initially. The company had stated that hackers had stolen around 70 million customers' name, address, phone number and e-mail address. Events such as these are throwing light on how there is still a massive threat to identity in a society, which is quite technologically advanced. These events highlight the need for stronger security measures.

Blockchain technology provides a potential solution to digital identity fraud and other issues. It does this by providing a unique authentication for every user ID on the network, which cannot be changed. The technology uses digital signatures for each user, which are based on public key cryptography. When authentication is conducted on the blockchain, only a single check is conducted, and this is whether the transaction was signed off using the correct key. The only caveat is that the system assumes that whoever enters the key is the rightful owner. So, you need to keep this private key very safely.

Blockchain Identity Use Cases

The technology of blockchains can be used in identity applications in the following areas:

- Passports
- Birth Certificates
- Vehicle registration
- E- residency
- Wedding certificates
- Digital identities
- IDs

ShoCard is a digital ID card that protects user privacy. It is as easy to use and understand as a driver's license. The identity is very secure, and so a bank can rely on it as well. The ID has been optimized for usage on mobile phones.

Smart Contracts

The term smart contract has been mentioned earlier in this book, but what exactly is it? Smart contracts are digital contracts that are legally binding. These contracts are uploaded on the blockchain network. What some developers do is implement these contracts as statements that can trigger the release of money using some cryptocurrency network (so far only the Bitcoin network has been used) instead of trusting an outside central authority.

For instance, if two users on the network want to exchange 500 dollars at some time in the future when some conditions are met, they would use a smart contract. The concept is very similar to the concept of futures in the financial market. When one of the users or both meets certain conditions, the exchange of funds takes place. Smart contracts are legally binding. They allow computers to take control of contracts and therefore make businesses more efficient and make the judiciary system stronger. Smart contracts can help in removing the need for trusting an intermediary for completing transactions. This can speed up processes immensely and make them safer.

Digital Voting

The world has been moving towards digitization, and the only obstacle to putting electoral processes on the Internet is the lack of security. However, using the blockchain technology, a voter could simply vote and submit it using their private key without ever revealing their real identity. The first time that a blockchain network was used to vote was in 2014 by a political party in Denmark called Liberal Alliance. Since voter turnout is still quite low in many countries including the United States, online voting might encourage the non-voters to start voting.

Decentralized Notary

There is another interesting feature associated with the blockchain technology called the **timestamp**. The entire network validates the state of some data (termed a hash) only at a certain time. Since the network is decentralized and there is no clear authority, this timestamp can be used to prove the existence of something at a certain time, and this can be used as a proof in a court of law as well. Up until this point, the only organizations that could provide this service were centralized notary services.

An Argentina based developer named Manuel Araoz built Proof of Existence, which is based on the concept explained in the previous paragraph.

How does Proof of Existence work?

Proof of Existence is a service that allows users to upload a file on the network and they need to pay a small transaction fee to obtain a cryptographic proof that it has been added to the blockchain. Once this is done, a hash of the file is generated and given to the user. The website for Proof of Existence shows the files that have been uploaded recently on the blockchain which have hashes. It uses the public ledger nature of the blockchain network to provide proof that your file exists on it. This can come in handy should any issues with authorship arise in the future.

This helps in circumventing the more expensive and time-consuming process of notarization. Since the world is moving to a value-based economy, systems that do not add value are discarded. There are many systems in today's world that are outdated and hinder the growth of the world. They do not add any value. Therefore, it makes sense to get rid of slower and less efficient systems such as centralized notaries. Using new and innovative technologies such as the blockchain technology can do this. The replacement of outdated systems with newer and more efficient ones will certainly speed up growth and can propel humans to heights that were never thought of before.

Chapter Nine: Understanding Bitcoins

The first chapters of the book cover all the information one would need to gather about blockchain technology and how it is used to secure the network used to transact cryptocurrencies. This would have led to understanding how cryptocurrencies like Bitcoins and Ethereum function. This chapter will give you a complete overview of Bitcoins and their importance in the current financial industry.

Bitcoin does not have a physical form like that of your traditional money such as dollars, rupees, pounds, etc. They are created and produced by solving complex cryptographic puzzles using hardware, which can help with high computational power and energy. There is no central authority or regulatory body to control the Bitcoin network, as they are completely decentralized. Bitcoins are produced when a transaction request is successfully verified thereby making it its payment network.

What is Bitcoin?

Bitcoin is the world's first and most popular cryptocurrency, which works on blockchain technology. It is also known as the virtual gold or referred as BTC for easy identification. Bitcoin is the digital money that can be held in an online wallet and can be used as a medium to exchange products or goods for its value without the need of a third-party intervention. The current traditional money transactions happen via third-party vendors such as central banks or government authorized financial institutions. With Bitcoin, the entire transaction takes place between the buyer and seller without any third-party intervention as the blockchain technology works on peer-to-peer electronic network concept.

It is a decentralized setup with a huge distributed central ledger that is used to track all the transactions that have ever happened in the history of that Bitcoin network thereby helping to keep the records up to date promptly. This is achieved by the blockchain technology. Bitcoin is completely based on mathematics and complex cryptography. Bitcoins can be produced when a complex mathematical problem (cryptographic puzzle) is solved using a certain set of procedures and protocols that work on a mathematical formula. This open source application is available for free on the Internet, and anyone can use the same.

How does Bitcoin work?

The blockchain is the distributed public ledger, which maintains the entire record of the complete transactional history that has happened in the network. When a new transaction request is generated, the said transaction is validated and verified using a process known as mining. Bitcoins are rewarded to the miners when the transaction verification process is successful. The authenticity of the transaction is secured by digital signatures, which in turn will be corresponding to the sending addresses. This will allow all the users in the network to send Bitcoins and control the same. The people who mine the Bitcoins are referred to as miners, and any Internet user with the required hardware can verify these transactions and become miners thereby getting rewarded with Bitcoins. All the confirmed transactions will be added to the blockchain.

When you install a Bitcoin wallet on your personal computer or mobile, you will get your first Bitcoin address that can be shared. A Bitcoin address can be used only once, and every time there is a new transaction, a new Bitcoin address will need to be generated. The transfer of value between Bitcoin wallets is referred to as a transaction, which also gets added in the blockchain when a transaction is verified and stamped as 'legitimate.'

To ensure that the transaction has indeed been sent by the 'actual sender,' a private key or seed is found in the Bitcoin wallet, which is used as a digital signature to make sure there is no security breach happening. Once the transaction request has been made, it is broadcasted to all the user nodes in the network. The miner confirms the transaction status in ten minutes and adds the new transaction block to the existing chain of the blockchain in chronological order to protect the network's neutral status.

This 'verification process' done by the miners plays an important role for the Bitcoins to be mined. Strict cryptographic protocols are followed to pack all the pending transactions into one block, which is then included in the existing chain of the blockchain. This is an irreversible process as once a transaction is confirmed there is no going back.

Bitcoin exchanges

There are different Bitcoin exchanges that users will need to choose from and most exchanges provide users with the option to store digital currency they hold. This function is the function of a bank account. Exchanges are the appropriate option for users trading in Bitcoins. This makes it easier for users to trade in Bitcoins since they do not need to give out any personal information when they make transactions.

The rules governing this trading are the same across different countries. No exchange has the authority to seize a user's Bitcoins. It is advisable to pick exchanges based on your location. Once a user creates an account, they need to link their bank account and follow some steps to allow the trading of Bitcoins.

Here is a list of some exchanges and where they operate from: Bitstamp operates out of the United States, Bitfinex operates out of Hong Kong, BTC-e and Kraken are also based in the US, Huobi operates out of China and Hong Kong, OKCoin and BTCC are also based in China. Coinbase can be used to trade in euros and US dollars.

Mining Bitcoins

One common way to obtain Bitcoins is to mine them. This is the process that is commonly followed. When you start mining Bitcoins, you need a computer to begin. Make sure you use a computer that has a good graphics card. Mining is now done in groups since it is easier to combine resources and start mining. The rewards obtained from mining in Bitcoins are shared among the miners according to a ratio that is always decided upon before the mining process begins.

Bitcoin investing strategies

Once you have understood how Bitcoins work and the different ways to make transactions with Bitcoins, you will need to understand how to invest in Bitcoins.

Always have a plan

Successful investors always have a plan before they begin investing in the stock market. They never improvise or follow their gut when they are investing in stocks. Users will need to identify a strategy they can follow when they begin investing in Bitcoins. You must always identify your end goal before you start investing in Bitcoins. You could choose to invest on a day-to-day basis or invest to save money for the future.

Price drops are common

The value of Bitcoins is volatile. The price of a Bitcoin could be extremely high on a given day but can drop drastically the very next day. These fluctuations are common for Bitcoins and occur more often when compared to stocks. If you are willing to invest in Bitcoins, you will need to expect changes in the value of the Bitcoin. Many financial experts are skeptical of investing in Bitcoins since they are unsure of how the fluctuating values will affect the existing system.

Don't forget to secure your Bitcoins

Bitcoin owners have undivided control over the money since Bitcoins are decentralized. Therefore, users must be careful and responsible when it comes to investing in Bitcoins. Users must be careful since they could cause their downfall. You can lose money by selling a Bitcoin at one of its lower rates if you do not expect the value of the Bitcoin to increase shortly. If there is a lapse in your security, you can be assured that another user may steal your Bitcoins. Users must be careful to keep their Bitcoins safe.

Conclusion

I want to thank you once again for purchasing this book.

Over the course of the book, you will gather all the information necessary for the blockchain technology. You will learn about how the blockchain technology came out and when it was created. The book also covers the benefits and limitations of the blockchain technology.

This technology is known to keep the cryptocurrency network safe by monitoring all transactions taking place. You will also learn about how this technology can be used in applications in the future. This technology is mostly used in the Bitcoin network since it was first used in the source code to create Bitcoins. You will also learn about Bitcoins and how one can invest in them. The advantages of using Bitcoins are the same as the blockchain technology since the technology is the foundation of the currency. Therefore, it is best to invest in Bitcoins currently.

I hope you have gathered all the information you are looking for.

Resources

https://www.coindesk.com/information/what-is-blockchain-technology/

https://hbr.org/2017/02/a-brief-history-of-blockchain

https://www.investopedia.com/terms/b/blockchain.asp

http://blog.ifsworld.com/2017/06/6-business-benefits-of-blockchain/

http://platformed.info/blockchain-and-the-new-face-of-decentralization/

https://hbr.org/2017/03/how-safe-are-blockchains-it-depends

http://www.dummies.com/personal-finance/10-rules-never-break-blockchain/

https://www.huffingtonpost.com/ameer-rosic-/5-blockchain-applications_b_13279010.html

https://www.coindesk.com/information/blockchains-issues-limitations/

https://www.investopedia.com/terms/p/private-key.asp

https://bitzuma.com/posts/six-things-bitcoin-users-should-know-about-private-keys/